DYSLEXIC LEGENDS ALPHABET

Words by Robin Feiner

A is for Dame **A**gatha Christie. Often called the 'slow one in the family,' Agatha struggled to read and spell as a child. But that didn't stop her from becoming the best-selling novelist of all time, with roughly two billion copies sold to date!

B is for Ann **B**ancroft. As the first woman to cross both polar ice caps to reach the South and North Poles, Bancroft's determination is legendary. Despite her challenges with dyslexia, she later became a teacher and now educates millions on the effects of global warming.

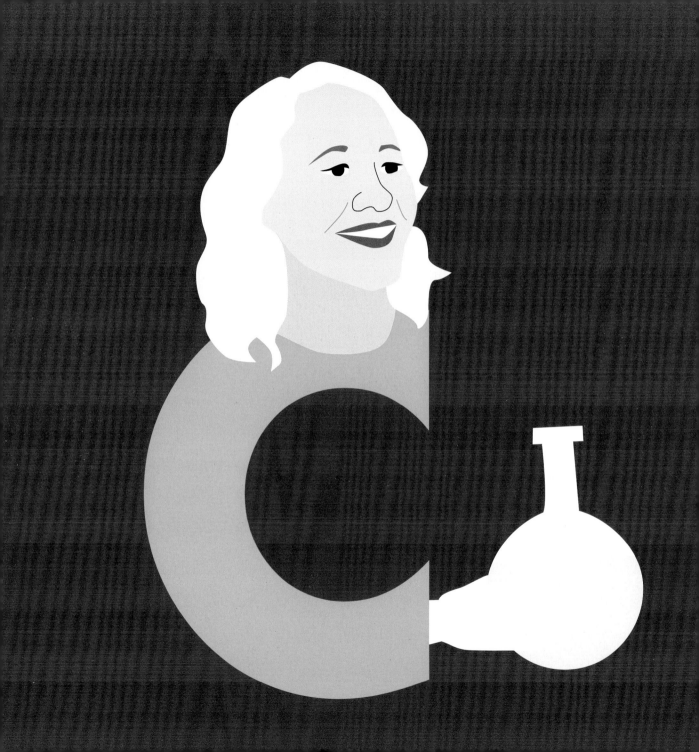

C is for Dr. Carol W. Greider. This distinguished professor and molecular biologist won the 2009 Nobel Prize in Physiology/Medicine. Dr. Greider credits dyslexia for her scientific success, claiming it helps her appreciate differences and make unusual decisions.

D is for Leonardo **d**a Vinci. For his legendary contributions to art, science, anatomy and invention, this renaissance man has been one of history's most forward thinkers – even if his notes were written in reverse!

E is for Albert Einstein.
This German genius discovered
the world's most famous
scientific formula and won
the Nobel Prize in Physics.
As a youngster, he experienced
learning difficulties and was
a very late talker – something
now often referred to as
'Einstein Syndrome.'

F is for Mick **F**leetwood. This self-taught drummer has been the driving force behind the legendary rock band, Fleetwood Mac, since 1968. Despite once being described as "a dreamer who didn't achieve academically," Mick went his own way to create an incredible career in music.

G is for Whoopi **G**oldberg. As a famous actress, singer-songwriter, comedienne, author, talk show host and political activist, Whoopi believes that dyslexia is often misunderstood. "We are not folks with a handicap, but folks with an interesting perspective on everything."

H is for Salma **H**ayek.
Her English was limited
and her dyslexia sometimes
confused matters even more,
but Hayek had her sights set
on Hollywood. Her beautiful
portrayal of legendary artist
Frida Kahlo in the 2002
movie 'Frida,' earned her
critical acclaim.

I is for John **I**rving.
With a National Book Award and an Academy Award to his name, you'd think that words came easily to this legendary storyteller. But Irving had to study twice as hard as others just to get through school.

**J is for Jamie Oliver.
While the Naked Chef is
a world-famous celebrity,
the naked truth is, he was
placed in special needs classes
at school. Jamie loved working
with his hands and soon found
his niche in the kitchen,
where his creativity began
bubbling over.**

K is for John F. **K**ennedy. Wrestling his dyslexia, JFK attended Harvard University, became a Pulitzer Prize-winning author and left his mark on history as the 35th U.S. President. He inspirationally once said, "Only those who dare to fail greatly can ever achieve greatly."

L is for John Lennon. Often a 'troublemaker' in the classroom, this Liverpudlian pursued music for self-expression and went on to become part of the most legendary band in history, The Beatles. He also continued to make trouble as an outspoken peace activist.

M is for **M**uhammad Ali.
In the boxing ring he could float like a butterfly and sting like a bee, but the greatest fighter there ever was didn't have the same confidence in the classroom. Ali later used his fame to help other African-Americans experiencing reading difficulties.

N is for **N**eil Smith.
At 6'4" and 273 pounds,
you wouldn't expect anything
to scare him, but Smith
certainly feared being called
on in class. Now, this two-time
Super Bowl champion inspires
other kids to tackle their
challenges head on through
the 'Yes I Can!' program.

Oo

O is for Octavia Spencer.
In addition to winning an
Academy Award and a Golden
Globe, this inspirational actress
has also written a series
of children's books. Spencer
credits her dyslexia for her
ability to solve problems
quickly and creatively.

Picasso

Pp

P is for Pablo Picasso. One of the most legendary painters of the 20th Century, Picasso often presented a back to front, out of order or turned and twisted world. We have dyslexia to thank for his wonderful and unique perspective on art and life.

Q is for **Q**uentin Tarantino. Despite a reported IQ of 160, Tarantino dropped out of high school in the ninth grade. His irreverence and taste for the unconventional have resulted in some of the most critically-acclaimed films of our time.

R is for Sir **R**ichard Branson. It's hard to believe that at the age of eight, he still couldn't read. And yet Branson has gone on to become a master entrepreneur, founding businesses that always break the mold. Thanks to this visionary, you may soon be able to go sightseeing in outer space.

S is for Steven **S**pielberg. This legendary filmmaker didn't let learning difficulties or relentless bullies stand in his way. It might take him twice as long to read a script, but the final picture is always a masterpiece.

T is for **T**homas Edison. America's greatest inventor began his education with hearing and learning difficulties. And yet we have him to thank for electricity, mass communication, sound recording and motion pictures. What a legend!

U is for Jørn **U**tzon. Suffering from dyslexia and dyscalculia, the young Dane knew engineering was not for him. But with an eye for geometry he became an architect, sculpting the majestic sails of the Sydney Opera House.

V is for Ludwig **v**an Beethoven. One of the most exceptional composers of the classical era had his teachers perplexed. Because he struggled to follow instructions, they said he would never compose a thing. How wrong they were. Beethoven composed nine renowned symphonies!

W is for Woodrow **W**ilson. Despite not learning the alphabet until the age of nine, and not being able to read until age 12, Wilson became a professor at Princeton, and eventually the 28th U.S. President! He was also proudly awarded the Nobel Peace Prize in 1919.

X is for Ale**x**ander Graham Bell. A learning disability didn't stop this legend from making a life-changing discovery. While experimenting with hearing devices to help his deaf mother and wife, he ended up inventing the telephone! Interestingly, he refused to have one in his study because he found it distracting.

Yy

Y is for Lee Kuan **Y**ew.
The founding father and first
Prime Minister of Singapore
governed for three decades,
transforming the nation into
one of the wealthiest in Asia.
Yew's family has contributed
in many ways to the Dyslexia
Association of Singapore.

Z is for Benjamin **Z**ephaniah. As a youngster, he was told that his poor reading ability was a result of his race, and that he would likely end up in prison. Zephaniah is now a poet, writer, musician and professor. He was also named as one of Britain's Top 50 post-war writers.

The ever-expanding legendary library

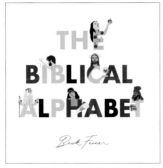

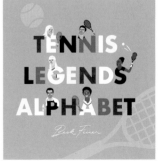

EXPLORE THESE LEGENDARY ALPHABETS & MORE AT WWW.ALPHABETLEGENDS.COM

DYSLEXIC LEGENDS ALPHABET

www.alphabetlegends.com

Published by Alphabet Legends Pty Ltd in 2019
Created by Beck Feiner
Copyright © Alphabet Legends Pty Ltd 2019

UNICEF AUSTRALIA

A portion of the Net Proceeds from the sale of this book
are donated to UNICEF.

9 780648 261681